This book is dedicated to everyone in the Project Management community and includes new and aspiring project managers.

INTRODUCTION

The contents of this book serve as a guide in addressing some practical or real-life aspects of project management that one would typically not see in a theoretical or academic setting. Each chapter is not a chapter in the real sense of the word. Rather, it is a possible scenario that is based on a real-life situation, and the primary purpose is to provide a response and a possible solution that may assist the project manager and his/her project.

It is based on my 15+ years experience in the IT project management industry. This is probably the first in the series of books that

I plan to release as a means to educate aspiring, new and experienced project managers. The primary goal is to offer my perspective and close the gap that exists between theoretical and practical project management experience.

I hope this book provides value to all those who want to make a career in project management and reap the benefits of understanding what they can expect when working on real projects. I believe this book will help project managers make a better transition into the work environment, perform well, and make it successful in the long run.

LEGAL DISCLAIMER

The author has made all reasonable efforts to provide current and accurate information for the readers of this book. The author and its associates will not be held liable for any unintentional errors or omissions that may be found. Any contents of this book is purely a personal opinion based on industry experience and should not be construed as the only response to the question being addressed.

The material in the book may include information by third parties. Third party materials comprise of opinions expressed by their owners. As such, the author of this book does not assume responsibility or liability for any third-party material or opinions.

The publication of third party material does not constitute the author's guarantee of any information, products, services or opinions contained within third party material. Use of third party material does not guarantee that your results will mirror our results. Publication of such third-party material is simply a recommendation and expression of the author's own opinion of that material.

Whether because of the progression of the

Internet, or the unforeseen changes in company policy and editorial submission guidelines, what is stated as fact at the time of this writing may become outdated or inapplicable at a later date. Great effort has been exerted to safeguard the accuracy and validity of this writing.

This book is copyright © 2018 with all rights reserved. It is illegal to redistribute, copy, or create derivative works from this eBook whole or in parts. No parts of this report may be reproduced or retransmitted in any forms whatsoever with the written expressed and signed permission from the author.

COPYRIGHT PAGE

Practical Project Management

By Raghu Ramasubbu

© 2018 Raghu Ramasubbu. All rights reserved.

No part of this publication may be reproduced, stored in a retrieval system, or transmitted in any form or by any means, electronic, mechanical, photocopying, recording, or otherwise, without written permission of the publisher.

Table of Contents

Pursuing a career in project management   8

Knowing the workplace environment   10

Knowing your project team members   13

Managing a project without end dates   15

Tools for project management   17

Your career path with Project Mgmt. Degree   19

Project Manager's role in defining the budget   20

Assignment of individuals to a project team   22

Manage a project without realistic schedule   24

Importance of project team member participation   26

True value of project status reports   28

Building and tracking to project schedule   30

Managing escalations on your project   32

Project failure and possible solutions   34

Risk management adoption in organizations   37

Managing Traditional and
Agile combined   39

Day and week in the life of a
project manager   41

Technical skills requirement
for a project manager   43

Project manager and release
management   45

Impact of scope change on a
project   47

Project manager philosophy
of control   50

Measure project manager
performance   54

Moving into a career in
project management   57

Managing conflict on project scope   59

Do project managers write project proposals?   61

Scope change leading to budget impacts   63

PMP versus Agile Certification   65

Task estimation on projects - challenges   66

The politics of managing projects   68

Theory versus practical project mgmt. - gaps   70

PMBOK adoption and practical project management   72

Future of project management	**74**
Project manager - skills & attributes	**76**
Organizational culture - impact on project manager	**78**
References	**79**

Pursuing a career in project management

The demand for project managers has significantly grown over the last few years, and it is still growing. Thanks to Project Management Institute (PMI) and the community that has been responsible for bringing about an awareness. Their goal is to promote the benefits associated with implementing the project and program management methodology in any type of organization that intends to manage work by projects.

If you are a fresh graduate coming out of college, it is most likely that you do not have the necessary certifications or work experience to make an entry into the world of project management. A good start would be to look for entry level project management opportunities in your current place of employment. In these positions, you usually work with a mentor that would train you to manage various aspects of a project.

It just means that you will get hands on experience as a project manager.

In addition to managing projects, you can pursue CAPM certification offered by the Project Management Institute (PMI). To qualify for the exam, you should have to accumulate 1,500 hours of project management experience or complete 23 hours of project management training as per PMI. The CAPM (Certified Associate in Project Management) certification helps you be recognized by companies that are looking to employ entry-level project management professionals. It is important to remember that at some point you will have to qualify and complete the PMP (Project

Management Professional) certification exam that has a more value in the project and program management world. As per PMI, you are eligible for this exam only after you have accumulated 4,500 hours of project management work experience.

If you are an experienced professional in other areas and want to move into project management, then the first step is to find project management opportunities in your current place of employment. At this time it is a good idea for you to pursue the CAPM certification because it will help you find employment in other organizations. Eventually, at some point, you have to get your PMP certification, that will carry you through and gain a foothold in the project management industry. Having functional and/or technical experience is definitely an advantage when it comes to project management work.

Finally, it is important to understand the nature of project management work. Learning and understanding the complexities of the job can help you determine if you want to make a career in project management. Today there is a host of online courses that may help you do the same and can also enhance or fine-tune your skills in the area of project management.

Knowing the workplace environment

If you are walking into a new organization as a project manager, that means you are starting off with a clean slate. You do not know the processes and tools nor the people with whom you are going to be working with. I can tell you from my 15+ years of experience as a project manager that you always start out from the ground up and experience does not really play a role in terms of how your performance is going to be measured.

Here is a list of things that you are likely to be involved during the first few weeks into the job:

- Assigned a workspace that is usually along with other project managers.
- You will be asked to review and understand company operations, policies, procedures, products and services so that you acquire some domain knowledge and organization profile. These days most of the information in on the company website.
- You will be introduced to departments, team members, project management office and also learn about reporting and communication protocols. You will have to know who is responsible for what part of

the project. The real challenge is to understand how all these departments/systems come together. Some companies publish a visual schematic usually on their intranet site that depict the organizational hierarchy and relationships.
- As you get more comfortable, you will get acquainted with the processes, tools and methodology related to managing projects. Your manager will also work on getting you access to various software tools that you need in order to do your job.
- Understanding all the systems and its interconnectedness is critical to your ability to manage a project, and that means you have to have an understanding of the

overall systems architecture that includes both hardware and software components.

- You would expect your manager or the PMO to provide you an orientation on project management reporting requirements and documents to be submitted and that could include weekly status reporting, creating and updating project plan, creating risks and issues document, and other documents as needed.
- It is also imperative that you reach out to your peers to get a better understanding of the daily, weekly responsibilities, processes, point of contact for specific tasks, current ongoing challenges, and documents to be prepared and submitted.

- Once you have been assigned a project by your manager, it is important to know your stakeholders and how they will be impacted by this project. Other things include identifying team members, a copy of the project charter if available and the expected deployment date on your project will help plan your work.
- When you host your first kickoff call on the project, it is official and you are the project manager responsible for the success or failure of the project. It is possible that you may be assigned multiple projects depending on your availability and the responsibilities, procedures, and processes discussed in the previous paragraphs still remain the same.

Knowing your project team members

One might imagine that this is the easiest part of the project but not necessarily because of the challenges and complexities involved. Organizations usually don't have a formal way of introducing you to team members and the leadership. Most likely you are going to be introduced to a few people with whom you will have very proximity due to project work. For others, you will have found your way through the maize by talking to your manager and other people in the organization.

It usually takes weeks if not months to get a full understanding of the organization structure and who are the primary points of contact for the groups involved. You will have to start walking around meeting people and introducing yourself. Many of them will usually be in meetings of some form or other and so it is not going to be easy to find time on their watch to introduce yourself and discuss each other's roles and responsibilities as related to your project.

You will also encounter remote workers who may part of your project team. Some of them you will get to know during the project kickoff call. Others, you will communicate with them through some form of instant messaging. Further, I would also include offshore resources as being remote workers. Offshore resources can pose communication challenges both from a cultural and process perspective and that will require some work as well.

In the midst of all this action, there are people who are leaving the organization and some new employees/contractors joining the organization. This is something you will have to keep track of as you manage your project because some of them may be part of your project team or have something to do with your project, maybe a critical resource.

It is not just enough that you know your project team members. As you move along the project life cycle, a relationship needs to be established so that work can be completed from each of the project team members. Often, this relationship is undervalued because the project manager makes an assumption that a team member contribution is only natural to project work and will not need much hand-holding, which is usually not the case.

Managing a project without end dates

As per PMI, "**projects are finite, which means they have a specific beginning and an end**"; otherwise it is considered maintenance work. Projects cannot go on forever. I am responding to this question only because it was asked in one of the blogs. I don't find this question to be realistic, but may be it is out there as a possible scenario that compelled me to address it in this book.

I am not sure how a project manager can manage a project without end dates. Why would an organization sponsor and execute a project, not knowing what and when something it needs to be delivered. It is difficult for a project manager to perform any kind of forward or backward planning without the project target end date. It is hard to imagine a project plan without a target end date and why would a sponsor fund a project that does not have an end date. Every project manager understands that this goes against the grain of fundamental project management.

In my view, managing projects without end dates is meaningless. As a project manager, I would be reluctant to take a project that does not have a target end date, because a target date is critical to project planning activity. It also means that the organization is not serious about project execution.

In such circumstances, the following questions need to be asked:

- What is the project charter and what is the overarching goal and purpose of the project?
- Does the organization have unlimited resources and money to keep going with the project? Also, the budget can only last for a certain period. A project has a finite budget, schedule, and scope.
- I would recommend that the project be locked into a release so that deployment

date is known, and project planning can be performed, keeping that target date in mind.

The project plan is the basis for any project management activity. Without a project plan, there is nothing to manage. It is the responsibility of the project manager to demand a target so that a project plan can be built out which would be the basis for tracking progress on the project. The project manager interacts with the stakeholders and the team members in order to develop that plan taking into account schedule, scope, and resource constraints.

In most cases, an organization publishes a release schedule for the year. Each of the release dates equates to a project end date. Any active project is assigned to a release date and is considered the project end date, when it is locked into that release. A project plan will include the release activities required to deploy the project. Many projects can be slotted into a release.

Tools for project management

Some standard tools used by a project manager are as follows:

- Microsoft Office
- Clarity
- Lotus Notes
- Microsoft Project
- In-house Project Management tool
- Cloud-based Project Management tool

In most organizations, Microsoft Office is the software of choice that is used for managing communications. It is the largest selling Office suite with most users and it is something most project managers are very much used to. Of course, there are exceptions where products like IBM Lotus notes or a cloud-based may be used to manage communications.

In the area of project management, Microsoft Project is popular primarily because of price and the potential discounts the organization gets from Microsoft. However, in licensing terms per user, it is still expensive and therefore many organizations prefer to build their own tools and customize it to suit their unique environment.

Cloud-based project management tools are getting popular these days because the organization has to pay to use the product whereas hosting and maintenance of the product is the responsibility of the vendor. This dramatically reduces the price per user cost and the cost of managing infrastructure is completely eliminated.

As a project manager, you will be surprised to note that there are companies that still use Microsoft Excel to create and manage plans. Some of these companies are more focused on milestones and budget and the enterprise level for tracking and reporting purposes. Tracking and managing detailed project plans is local to the project manager and really does not matter what tool they use, so long as the project manager reports out the big picture.

Your career path with Project Mgmt. Degree

If you are obtaining a project management degree, I am guessing you are looking to switch to a project manager role and grow from there. If that is the case, then you should pursue CAPM or PMP certification (offered by Project Management Institute; www.pmi.org), because that has become a prerequisite for project management job opportunities.

To qualify for the certification exam, you need to have 1500 hours of project management experience for CAPM and

3500 hours for PMP. You can also qualify for the CAPM exam with your project management degree because you can show 23 hours of project management training from the classes you have already taken. In terms of salary expectations by location, you can find information on sites like Glassdoor.com and Indeed.com.

If your current employer has entry level project management opportunities, you could try to apply for that position. You may also be lucky to find some entry level positions with other employers, from where you can build up your project management career. Definitely, approach IT recruiters in your area as they might have some opportunities for you as well and provide you guidance in terms of entry level project management opportunities.

Project Manager's role in defining the budget

Companies usually hire project managers to execute projects once the budget and the project charter has been reviewed and approved by the project management office(PMO) and/or the stakeholders. The PMO also employs a group of project managers whose primary function is to work on proposals, processes and performance metrics. They also keep a tab of active projects to make sure they are on track with respect to scope, schedule, cost, performance, and quality.

In some cases, project managers are assigned to work on project proposals, and also assist management on budget and business approvals, which is usually part of another group called the project pipeline management. This usually happens prior to the start of a project. Remember, a project can start only after it has received business and financial approvals.

It is important to highlight that project contract and procurement management are also part of the project management function. The guidelines and methodology are well documented in the PMBOK for project managers to learn about them. This function in most cases is the sole responsibility of the vendor management group within an organization, and works on negotiating and finalizing contracts with external vendors and contractors.

A project manager is likely to communicate the estimated cost on the project after the requirements are locked in. This cost can either be lower than, equal to or greater than the original budgeted cost of the project. The project manager faces a real challenge to convince the PMO and the stakeholders, only when the estimate exceeds the approved budget. This can happen for a variety of reasons, but getting the approvals needs justification and proof of data. If the extra money is not approved, it just means the project manager has to find creative ways to get the job done and it could mean reducing resources, cutting scope, optimizing task estimates to name a few. If the additional money is approved, then the project will create a formal change request to add that cost to the project.

Assignment of individuals to a project team

The pace of projects and its implementation has increased exponentially over the years due to competition in the online space. An organization is actively involved in developing new applications and at the same time maintaining and enhancing current working applications. This leads to severe resource constraints because of the pressures to develop new applications and maintain current ones at the same time. The goal of any organization is to limit resources on projects and maintain maximum throughput.

This leads to the question as to how resources are managed across projects. It is very common for a team member to be working on multiple projects. These team members are assigned to work on specific projects based on their skills, current load and work projections for the future. The leader of each team is responsible for managing resource utilization and to allocate buffer time that is necessary to support emergency requests.

As a project manager, one is going to deal with team member participation issues in project meetings. Resources allocated to multiple projects is going to cause contention and that is something all project managers are going to deal with. In order to get the resource attention, the project manager might be forced to host separate meetings or communicate via email and/or instant messaging to meet the needs of the project. The stakeholders expect the project manager to have full control and latest information on the project. Any gaps as such is considered to be poor project management. Resource contention can become a risk on the project and will need to be escalated to get the attention of the stakeholders. As a project manager, it is important to know how and when resource contention or constraint is going to affect the assigned tasks in the project plan.

Manage a project without realistic schedule

The title assumes that the project manager has already built out the plan that includes tasks, subtasks and the resource assignments. The project manager has determined that based on task completion estimates and resource availability, it is difficult to meet target dates as determined by business stakeholder expectations. The decision to deploy an application or a service on a certain date is usually based on market competition and time to market considerations. The following are some options available to the project manager:

- Work with the team leads to determine if additional resources are available.
- Work with team leads and members to determine if the task can be completed earlier than current estimates.
- Work with architects and team lead to determined if anything can be used from previous projects to reduce development time.
- Some teams may be able to reduce total effort on the project to bring in the project on time. For example, the testing team may be able to reduce the total number of test cases to be tested or even use automated scripts to bring down the overall testing time.

- If none of the previous options work, then discuss with reporting manager and stakeholders to explain the situation. Remember that evidence is required through data points in order to convince the stakeholders about the potential schedule constraint in delivering the project. This may lead to a possible reduction in scope, which would then help maintain the schedule on the project.
- The project manager needs to host a call and place the options on the table so that he/she can gain consensus on mitigating the schedule constraint. In most cases, the option to delay the project is not really an option. The stakeholders expect

the project manager to find a way to meet the schedule. It may also require to re-prioritize projects so that the critical ones get the resources needed. It requires the responsibility of the business and the PMO to help with prioritization and determine what needs to go in first as a means to support the business.

Importance of project team member participation

Resource constraints leading to an increased workload is a hallmark of today's workplace environment. Furthermore, you will notice that there are too many meetings in a workday and the team members have to make a choice on which ones to attend. They also need time to get their job done and that is the primary contention that we are addressing here. Technical folks at times have a very negative mindset and do not see the value of project management as a driving force in getting the project completed successfully. Rather they see this as an overhead and a hindrance to completing their work.

The management is most organization believes that project management is the cost incurred to complete and deploy projects on time and within the budgeted cost. In other words, it is the cost of doing work and an integral part of project success in an organization. That is a reason organizations have moved to managing by projects in order to produce goods and services on a timely basis to beat the competition. At the same time, organizations have come to believe the true value of project and program management.

In order to solve this issue, the project manager must call out teams and/or individuals who are not attending the meeting or reporting out status. A one-on-one discussion can be the starting point and if that does not work, it is recommended that a formal escalation is raised to the department head and to the reporting manager so that they are aware of the problem. This may be followed up with face to face or virtual meetings to find a solution to the problem and the best way to get the team member engaged on the project.

Project managers should not underestimate the nature of the problem. Attending meetings and reporting meetings are an integral part of a project manager's success and therefore without it there is nothing to manage. This is the communication aspect of project management and is critical to measuring project progress, mitigating issues and risks, and taking action as necessary. It is also a source of key project information that will be presented to the stakeholders on a regular basis.

It is the responsibility of the project manager to ensure that each of the team members is working closely with other project team members and any issues that arise are clearly addressed on a timely basis. It is important for the project manager to build some confidence within the team and reinforce the idea that each member's contribution and participation is valuable and critical to the success of the project. That means keeping the morale up within the project team is critical to getting quality work done on time and within budget. It is the responsibility of the project manager to set expectations for the team so that participation is not optional.

True value of project status reports

Based on what I have seen, the weekly status report is a lot of work and something that people never have time to read. It is a document that provides a weekly snapshot of project progress. As long as the project is making good progress, the management usually does not interfere much and that is a great testament to trusting the project manager. However, when a project runs into problems, all eyes are on the project and the project manager, and that means more engagement will be required by the project manager to justify and explain the current status.

In an age of information overload, if a team member and stakeholders actively involve themselves in the project, there is absolutely no need for a project status report. So long as the project manager is able to provide a snapshot in the weekly status call, that should be enough to keep people informed on project progress.

Free time is a luxury for most in the organizational resources. The weekly status report that is usually multiple pages long and should be converted to a single slide so that team members and stakeholders get a view of the progress without having to spend too much time reading it. Most of them are always focused on risks and issues because those are the items that can jeopardize project progress. If the project is in "green" status, there is nothing to discuss other than plans for next week. Some project managers discuss accomplishments in the project report and that is a good thing in order to recognize team members.

For many project management organizations (PMO), the need for a weekly status report is more of a formal process that seeks to capture information for future audit if necessary. That document once archived can be used as a historical reference to future projects, but is never the case because of the sheer amount of information that needs to be managed. If the management and the sponsors can find more efficient ways to determine project progress, that will be a good way to save cost incurred on preparing weekly reports. There are tools in the market that can generate reports at one-third of the cost assuming the project manager can keep the information up to date in the tool of choice.

In addition, the work overhead increases exponentially when additional reports are requested asking for the same information in a various other formats. As a result, the project manager spends less time managing the project activities needed to make progress. In my view, if the stakeholders and the PMO can find efficiencies with project status reporting, it will help the project manager focus on project execution.

Building and tracking to project schedule

Analysts, architects, and developers are trained to perform their specific tasks, but they are not trained to think like a project manager. While the project manager is always focused on planning for tasks, schedule and cost on a project, analysts and developers are more focused on executing work. Even if the teams provide details of their progress, there are always issues with identifying tasks that have been completed and/or work-in-progress. They are not trained to estimate and therefore the burden falls on the project manager to make it all look consistent and accurate.

When the project is in progress, one will be caught off guard by things that were not communicated during the project planning phase. Because they are executing multiple tasks in parallel for various projects, it is possible that the estimated completion date may completely vary from the original dates provided to the project manager. It is the project manager's responsibility to get an understanding of the task details and in what order they are going to be completed.

In my 16 years experience as a project manager, I have noticed that teams have different ways and formats for estimating and managing tasks. There is no one standard approach and that makes it difficult for the project manager to consolidate all the information into one cohesive project plan. Project managers often struggle to figure out completed tasks, items that are still work in progress and tasks that have been completed. Managing tasks to dates coupled with complex communication requirements make the job very hard, catching the project manager off guard in many instances. If each of the project team do their reporting responsibilities correctly, then the project manager does not have to reach out again and again for clarifications.

In my opinion, there is not a single answer to this problem. One has to be patient and work very closely with the teams to get an understanding of the sequence of work, dependencies, dates, risks, and issues. One important thing to remember is that development teams do not see risk and issues the same way the project manager does and that requires working closely with them to come with a consensus on project status at any point in time. For example, when reporting a project as "red" or "yellow" department heads are likely to push back and that is something that should be managed politically by the project manager.

Managing escalations on your project

When you are new to the organization, it is imperative that you understand the organizational structure and the chain of command. First few weeks into the job, you should get an understanding of the communication structure from your manager or your peers. Sometimes that information is hard to find because there is not any formal document that addresses this. It is very likely that the information is published on the company's website . I typically use information from the intranet site to understand who is who and the reporting hierarchy. You can also try talking to your peers and team members to get specific information. As you learn more, it is a good idea to document them for the benefit of the project and your own sanity.

If you are a seasoned employee, you should have figured out by now how the escalation process works. Here are some things you can do to manage project-related escalations:

- Always work with your manager. Make sure he/she knows the problem before you actually escalate the issue to the project teams and key stakeholders. Your manager may take

a proactive approach to solving the problem even before it gets to the project risk meeting.
- Most project based organizations usually host a weekly call to talk about issues, risks and how to mitigate them. This is the next best place to escalate the problem after you have notified your reporting manager.
- If the problem is specific to a team, you can first escalate the problem to the team lead and try to address it that way, before it gets to the weekly risk call.
- The project management organization and the key stakeholders are always concerned about projects moving from

green to yellow or red status. This requires the project manager to act on it with a sense of urgency before it is escalated to the higher levels.

- The project manager has to be cognizant of what and what should not be escalated. If the project manager can resolve the issue, that is the best option in order to reduce visibility and concern at the management and stakeholder level.
- Managing escalations appropriately also requires some political savvy. The project manager should understand the nature and sensitivity of the issue, discuss with the reporting manager, before making it known to the larger

group. I have seen cases where a risk associated with my project was completely rejected during the weekly call only because some of the senior members did not agree that it was a risk. At times there was a sense that the risk was being rejected only because those handful of people did not want to look bad in front of the senior management.

Project failure and possible solutions

Project failure can manifest in the many forms. It just means that the goals of the project have not been met. Every project has a project charter that documents the goals and expectations of a project and that forms the basis to determine if a project is a success or failure.

SCOPE IMPACT

The project did not meet the full scope of what was originally committed on the project. Many organizations may claim success even if the scope was changed and/or reduced, but if it did not meet the core requirements without which that product or service cannot function, then it is considered a project failure. Therefore delivering required scope is critical to project success.

SCHEDULE IMPACT

The project manager builds out a schedule once the tasks and time estimates are received from the project team. This should give a sense of whether all of this can be accomplished within the time planned or promised. If there are issues and/or risks, the project manager works to mitigate them ahead of time to avoid any late surprises that could jeopardize the project. It could mean things like ADDING RESOURCES, REDUCING SCOPE, INCREASING BUDGET etc.

COST IMPACT

The project manager should be able to arrive at a project cost using the project schedule, resource count, and resource rate. If the project cost is greater than the approved budget, the project manager must to go back to the sponsors for additional money. If that is rejected, then the project manager will have to negotiate with the project teams and partners. If that does not work, then the project manager must look at reducing scope as the last option or cutting back on resources.

QUALITY IMPACT

Quality of the final product and/or service can also have an impact on project success. Break fixes are usually done during the Quality Assurance phase, but it may be too late if the team finds too many defects. So the quality of development and unit testing is critical to product/service deployment. In any case, the defects will be fixed post-production after which the product/service will be launched in the market. If the team does not deliver a quality product/service to the market, then that can be considered product and project failure.

PROJECT MANAGER PERFORMANCE IMPACT

Equally important is the quality of the project manager. It is all about tracking to schedule, cost and scope, controlling the project, and to mitigate risks and issues on a timely basis.

RESOLUTION RECOMMENDATIONS

- Apply the concept of triple constraint, and make sure the scope is realistic in relation to cost and schedule. That means the project manager will have to cut scope. One or more of the constraints may have to be adjusted to meet project goals.

- Classify the requirements into MUST HAVE, NICE TO HAVE and low priority items from a business standpoint. Talk to the stakeholders about focusing on the MUST-HAVES. That will give the project manager control over delivering the project on time and within budget.
- Remember anticipating risks and mitigating them as quickly as possible is also critical to project success. That means timely escalations, calling out teams on risks and finding solutions is the approach to eliminating possible project failure in the future.

Other things that may impact a project and will need resolution are:

- Poor quality of requirements and/or design.
- Lack of synergy within the project team.
- Not enough resources available to support the project.
- Resource skills not adequate.
- Poor and inaccurate estimates.
- Gaps in scope clarity between the project team and business stakeholders.
- Failure of the vendor to meet contractual obligations.

Risk management adoption in organizations

Most project-based organizations, take risk management seriously to the extent of escalation and mitigation. However, based on the PMBOK guide, the processes, tools, and template are far more advanced compared to what is typically applied in organizations. For most organizations, the process looks like this based on my experience:

- PMO creates a shared document, usually an XL sheet to assist project managers to post risks and issues associated with their projects.

- A weekly risk meeting is hosted by the PMO where project managers are expected to talk about their project and provide guidance on the potential impacts and how the project manager is going to resolve the open risk and/or issue.
- If the risk/issue prolongs for some period, say weeks, then it can attract concern and visibility.
- If the risk/issue or closed, then it is archived and removed from the document.
- The weekly meeting continues until the week prior to the release.

While the PMBOK document provides guidelines for managing project risk, most of the tools and techniques provided by the document is rarely used. It is highly likely that someone in the PMO has documented the methodology and posted it on the website, but my point is none of that is taken literally or seriously. In my view, here are some things that are important and never taken into consideration.

- Risk management implementation document.
- Probability and Impact matrix.
- Qualitative and Quantitative methods and tools thereof.

- Stakeholder Risk Tolerance matrix.
- Detailed Risk register.

In my view, risk has always been a sensitive issue and a source of contention across all groups within the organization. For example, the project manager might consider something as a risk to the project and another team will disagree with it. Sometimes the reporting manager does not agree to something as being a risk because he/she would look bad in the eyes of the PMO and the management.

Most of the delivering groups take that mentality, and so when the risk becomes an actual issue, everyone is scrambling and blaming each other. At this point, the blame game becomes very political and the most powerful person wins. You as a project manager might end up looking bad because the game was not played correctly (in a political sense) to the satisfaction of the PMO.

To conclude, proper risk management requires transparency and trust and the ability to be open about current and future issues on a project.

Managing Traditional and Agile combined

From a project manager's perspective it is a challenge because the teams that follow the traditional approach are going to have a schedule that is very different from the agile team. Let us look at the difference.

TRADITIONAL/WATERFALL:
- Analysis
- Design
- Development
- Testing
- Deployment

AGILE
- Sprint (2 or 4 weekly cycle)
  - Development
  - Testing
  - Deployment
  - Customer validation

It is important to remember that in terms of the schedule, teams following the traditional/waterfall approach is the long pole in the tent. Until those teams complete the development, the work from the agile teams cannot be integrated into the final product. In my view, it is not ideal or productive to have an agile team inside of the traditional/waterfall model. Rather, agile should be implemented in places where the work is independent of the larger/longer waterfall project. Their work should not depend on a team that is following the traditional/waterfall model and vice versa because they do not align well in terms of methodology and schedule. However, there are companies that follow the hybrid approach as a means to make an entry into the agile world, making compromises on cost and schedule if necessary.

I am sure there are agile frameworks that help support such a hybrid model, but how far that is going to be successful, considering all aspects of project management remains to be determined. My argument is that when the methodology is completely different between teams on a single project, the likelihood of issues/risks is exponentially greater.

Day and week in the life of a project manager

Here are a list of activities that the project manager is likely to do or be involved in on any day/week during the life of a project. The ones mentioned as WEEKLY could be on any of the working days. This list may not encompass everything, but most of them are accounted for.

- Attend team meetings (DAILY) as needed.
- Project status team meeting. (WEEKLY)

- Review emails that are important or critical from a project perspective. (DAILY)
- Update/ Review project schedule and determine what is coming up for completion the current week. Applies to all phases of the project. (WEEKLY)
- Contact teams to confirm the completion date plus any issues or risks that the project manager should know. (WEEKLY)
- Document/review new and current risks respectively and make updates as necessary. Maybe even close the risk/issue as needed. (WEEKLY)
- Review/update project task list if changes have to be made. (WEEKLY)

- Review actuals versus budget and determine if there could be risk of budget overrun. (WEEKLY)
- Update project status/schedule based on the project meeting. (WEEKLY)
- Attend PMO meeting to provide overall project status. (WEEKLY)
- Attend risk meeting to discuss risks/issues/mitigation on the project. (WEEKLY)
- Management meeting to discuss achievements, accomplishments, issue etc. (WEEKLY)
- If an external vendor is involved, then a weekly meeting would include them as well.

- Preparing project status report and submitting to PMO and other key stakeholders usually at the end of the week. (WEEKLY).
- Meeting with the reporting manager to discuss progress, risks, issues etc.(WEEKLY)

Technical skills requirement for a project manager

There are three categories of project managers. They are as follows:

- Generalist
- Functional
- Technical

A generalist is someone who is an expert in project management and has a good knowledge of the project management methodology. The functional project manager has general skills and experience in one of the verticals such as telecommunications, finance, insurance to name a few. A technical project manager is one who has general skills along with good knowledge of specific technology platforms, architecture, product etc.

Based on personal experience, I would say that being a technical project manager is the best option assuming he/she has an opportunity to work on specific technology or platform. The odds of success in the job market increase if the experience includes both project management and strong technical skills. Many companies do hire functional project managers because the technical needs of the project are managed by the architects and developers. A project manager who is a generalist can play an advisory role, but is not the preferred choice in most organizations due to lack of functional and technical experience.

As in my case, I have been a functional project manager all along only because I was never exposed to technology and the job responsibility never required to be one. So if you were an architect in your previous life and then plan to move to project management, you are in a great position to find a job. Look at the job description for project management positions today, one will notice that a lot of emphasis is given to technical knowledge and experience.

So if you are a generalist and/or a functional project manager, I would recommend that you take online or instruction based courses to get to know and learn products and platforms, and how they are implemented. I also want to emphasize that this applies to both traditional, waterfall and agile project management.

Project manager and release management

Companies that manage work by doing projects develop a release or deployment schedule for the year. Projects get deployed into production based on a defined release schedule. The deployment is a combination of new products, application enhancements, data center work etc. Companies normally plan 3-4 big releases each year and a few small releases to support minor work.

Once a project has been approved and assigned to a project manager, the project sponsor and/or the reporting manager will communicate to the project manager about the planned release schedule. The project will be slotted into that release schedule, and when creating the project plan, it should align with the release milestone created for that schedule. Multitude of projects are assigned to a release. It is very much possible that the success or failure of one project may have an impact on the success or failure of another project, with both going into the same release.

As a project manager, you are not only tracking your project but also working with other project managers and the release manager to track the dependent projects.

Also, remember that any issue or risk on one project may jeopardize your project and sometimes the release as a whole. In other words, there are a lot of moving parts across projects that are tied together in order to make the release successful.

It is obvious from the previous paragraphs, that the role of a project manager is much more than just managing his/her project and that makes it even more complex. The project teams are multi-tasking and they have to balance out the needs of all the project teams assuming everyone has resource constraints which in most cases is always true given the volume of work that needs to be completed. The project manager should also keep a tab on other dependent projects and work with other project managers to make the release successful.

As an FYI, release management is a sub-component of the IT Service Management Framework that is popularly known as ITIL, and it is the acronym for Information Technology Infrastructure Library.

Impact of scope change on a project

Change is inevitable and the only thing that is certain is change. While we can all agree to this, it is imperative that all project managers understand the impact of scope changes to projects that are in the pipeline or in the execution phase. As project managers, the formal approval of functional & system requirements and design in an indication that we are ready to build out the product/service followed by testing and implementation.

Now consider the impact on your project when the business model changes with the organization. These business changes can have cascading impacts on the various phases of the project. From a project scope perspective, these business changes can force the stakeholders to rethink the requirements and design for the product or service being developed. Let me attempt to define the potential impacts:

- Modify business requirements to include new scope followed by changes to business and function requirements.

- Impact to current approved design, which means changes to product or service architecture.
- Depending on the level of impact the project may have to canceled.
- Modifications to requirements and design could result in the creation of additional change requests to support scope, schedule and cost impacts.
- If the scope impacts are significant the project, then the request may go back to the pipeline process for business justification, re-estimation and funding approvals.

As project managers, we all should be ready for potential changes to our projects. When the industry is disruptive, the organization that is impacted is forced to re-evaluate its strategic goals and objectives leading to changes in the tactical plan. Active projects are re-evaluated as a result to see if it makes sense to continue with scope changes or abandon them for good. In today's world, the speed of business change is so fast that it inevitably puts programs and projects at risk on an ever-increasing basis.

During my tenure as a project manager and in my experience I have noticed that schedule and cost changes are cascading impacts resulting from scope changes to a project. I have rarely seen scope changes from schedule or cost impacts. I am not trying to say that such scenarios cannot or will not happen. Given the fact that scope, schedule, and cost form the triple constraint for a project, other scenarios are likely but very rare in occurrence although many may not agree to it.

To clarify my point, business stakeholders have never approached me to cut scope in order to meet cost and schedule requirements and maybe that is the mindset in the work environment.

It is also very important to highlight that the quality of scope management has a direct bearing on the quality of business requirements. Project team members often complain that the customer has not clearly laid out the business requirements in an effort to develop quality functional and system requirements. So when additional change requests are created for a project, it is often an indication that there is scope creep because of poor business requirements.

The quality of good business requirements can also be a subjective thing only because each customer has a different style of writing unless a tool can be used to standardize such content. Business requirements can be also be supported by developing use case scenarios to better articulate the needs of the project in very clear terms so that the project team members can understand and execute to that outcome.

It is also important to remember that the quality of a project diminishes with increasing scope creep. This not only impacts schedule and cost components of the project but the overall quality of the expected deliverables of the project. For example, if a project life cycle stretches on due to scope changes, it may reach a point where the project becomes irrelevant and does not meet the original purpose for which it was intended.

Project manager philosophy of control

When one talks about control, it is possible to draw parallels between the project management function and being a "control freak", I am just curious at this point if a good project manager imbibes some characteristics of a "control freak". If one looks at the PMI definition of a project management, one of the project processes does address the concept of control. Well, the control part of the process is quite different from the control I am talking about something associated with a personality type. The general assumption that a project manager should have responsibility and control over his/her project is convincing enough to make the claim in my view.

However, as a general observation, the word "control freak" has a negative connotation in a psychological context while it is a prerequisite for a successful project outcome. Referring to the definition provided by Google, the word "control freak" is defined as follows:

"A person who feels an obsessive need to exercise control over themselves and others and to take command of any situation." (https://www.google.com/?gfe_rd=ssl&ei=dHaNVrORPM2F-AWxnZu4CA#q=meanin

g+of+control+freak)

There is the expectation that the project manager directs and guides the project to a successful outcome. The question is what if you are not comfortable with being a "control freak" in the context of project management based on one's personality type? Why would you choose such a profession? Would it be only to please your ego? If anyone disagrees with the notion, then what is the level of control needed for a successful project manager? Does the personality type even address the concept of "control" as an attribute?

I am asking this question only because we

are often criticized for being control freaks in our personal lives and I think in this case it is only human nature that we all have some amount of it. I would agree that each one of us would definitely like to have some control over our lives, but what about control over others or events, which is something I am sure we will all cherish and something that allows us to exert influence. At times we may also deny and deceive ourselves about the fact that we are not controlling or influencing anyone. Obviously, the word "influencing" has a much more positive connotation in the eyes of many, coupled with underlying motives.

In job interviews, I am often asked about

projects that I believe were successful and unsuccessful. While it is true that there are many factors for project success, I wanted to seek answers to the concept of "control" and is that based on training and/or personality. Every aspect of project management whether is scope, schedule, quality or performance needs some level of control and playing that game requires someone who loves control and is not threatened by it. In an organization setting, control is what drives goals and outcome as people think fit in their chain of command. This is also a source of conflict when there is a clash over what, when and how something needs direction and control to reach a certain expected outcome.

As per the thesaurus dictionary, some words that are considered opposite of control and they are as follows: Chaos, disorganization, freedom, lawlessness, mismanagement, neglect, advantage, inability, weakness, helplessness, powerlessness, relinquishment, and renouncement.

Well, it is obvious that some of the words that I have highlighted are consequences of poor project execution managed and mitigated during the life cycle of the project. In my experience, there have been many cases where projects have deviated from its original plan, most likely due to business changes. In those circumstances, it is unreasonable to assume that the project manager did not have adequate control over the project outcome. This only means that business sponsors have a stake in the game in terms of controlling what comes in as changes and scoped into the project so that it meets the deadlines as originally planned for the project. At the same time, it is a moot point to deploy that project because the functionality being deployed may not support the new or modified business model.

We should be aware of the fact that we must not stifle creativity in the name of control. As project managers, we could potentially see ourselves controlling or discouraging the very expressions and ideas that might translate to better project outcome, something we may never know because of our habitual nature. Therefore developing the best solution that is beneficial to the business is better said than done because there is this notion of personal achievement on top of accountability and responsibility, which drives control to even greater level.

A project manager is also a leader who is directing and guiding the project team to a certain expected outcome. Therefore it is automatically assumed that control is a critical part of that leadership. It is conclusive that leadership and control also has a very tight relationship because control is one of the key attributes of successful leadership. The control function is also at the core of leadership and we could very well say "project manager = leader = control" which essentially means that a project manager should also be a leader to direct and guide the team to success. Only when a project manager has leadership capabilities, can he/she be able to control the project outcome. The question is whether a project manager can learn the art of control or is it something that is a part of his/her personality calls for further analysis and discussion.

Measure project manager performance

I have been working to design a framework or template for measuring project manager performance. This effort was associated with some new recruits and to gauge how well they are performing in the first few months on their job. Soon I realized that the roles and responsibilities of a typical project manager automatically lend itself to developing those measurement factors quickly and easily and something that focuses on project outcome.

My goal was to put this in front of the

audience so that it can assist other project managers with a framework that they can use. At the same time, it can also serve as a guide identifies factors that can used to improve project manager performance. Allow me to present those attributes with a little bit of detail. My hope is that this may start a conversation and bring about further ideas from other experienced project managers as a means to educate all of us in the hope of excelling in the field of project management and something all project managers do for a living.

Following are some of the critical parameters that could be used to measure project manager performance.

So what are the parameters for measurement:
- Understanding of project objectives and stakeholder needs.
- Facilitation and management of team meetings.
- Effectively lead a team.
- Communication effectiveness: emails, reports, metric etc.
- Effective planning, tracking and control.
- Manage risks and issues on a project.
- Ability to meet deadlines and deliverables.

- Make timely decisions and solve problems effectively.
- Actively seeks and provides feedback.
- Effectively uses project management tools.
- Actively contributes and participates in meetings, discussions.
- Actively seeks to understand domain knowledge and processes.

How you measure them is something that is purely up to you and your organization. However, one approach that I can suggest is based on a range of values and weights factored below:

Values 1-5 (1-low 5-High)

VERY SATISFIED	SATISFIED	MODERATELY SATISFIED	DISSATISFIED	VERY DISSATISFIED

Another question that one might ask is the length and frequency of project manager performance measurement. It can be an ongoing effort or can be done for a specific duration. The other question would be related to how the attribute values are going to be captured. In my view, the project sponsor is probably the best candidate to observe and capture the information because they have the biggest stake in the project compared to anyone else on the team. Of course, in order to get a more realistic view using a population, one can send this out to multiple stakeholders for feedback that may help remove any bias that might exist.

Considering how quickly the framework can be developed, the longest and hardest part of the measurement is related to capturing of data using a live project and putting them all together in a coherent single view to analyze. Stakeholder feedback is critical to any project and so is project manager performance, that is directly tied to project outcome and acceptance criteria.

In the same manner, this framework could be used for internal assessment as well and that will again need some form of observation coupled with face to face interviews to get a better sense of performance using goals, expectations and the resultant outcome. Many companies do have performance reviews that are more HR centric and is not really related to project management performance.

To conclude, I would restate the earlier fact that project manager performance is critical to the success of any project and some parameters include good communications, leadership, articulate, accountable, proactive to name a few. As a project manager, one can use this framework for their personal success.

Moving into a career in project management

In theory, it is possible if you have a good amount of experience in project management. Everyone would agree that real life project management experience is much more valuable than advanced education and/or certification. One may have a Master's degree related to project management. However, without experience, it might be difficult to get an entry-level job in project management. There are companies that do recruit project management interns with an MS degree, but it may be hard to find such opportunities.

The job situation for aspiring project managers is different today. Irrespective of whether you have experience or not, CAPM or PMP certification has become mandatory to get a foot in the door. Recruiters or talent acquisition specialists eliminate job applications for those that do not have the CAPM or PMP certification. In many organizations including the Federal Government, PMP certification has become mandatory and a prerequisite for project manager position.

Today, there is a significant demand for project managers with agile experience. A few years ago, the Project Management

Institute(PMI) launched a new certification exam called PMI-ACP that is focused on agile project management. There are other certifications in the market such as Certified Scrum Master (CSM), Agile SAFe etc that also carry equal weight when it comes to agile related jobs.

While many consider agile to be the future of project management, I can say with certainty that traditional project management jobs are here to stay for a while. Agile has not reached maturity to handle large and complex projects and especially those that include infrastructure development and deployment. Today agile development is mostly used in organizations that design and develop software products, and startups are usually the ones to adopt this methodology.

Managing conflict on project scope

Critical to a project kickoff is a signed and approved project charter. A project charter is important precisely to solve the question that is being presented. A project charter defines the vision, scope, and expectations of the project and is the basis for moving to the next phase of the project.

In my experience, there have been instances where I started a project with no formal project charter in hand. In this case, I had to rely on the business requirements and stakeholder sign-off to get to the next phase of the project and to use those requirements to lock in the scope of the project.

The requirements phase provides an opportunity for the stakeholders to formalize their vision and the expectations of the project. Once this is formally reviewed and approved by the stakeholders it is all is good to move forward to the next phase of the project. Once the project moves past the requirements phase, any changes to scope will be handled via a project scope change request process.

Once the requirements are signed off by the business, there should not be any conflict with respect to vision and expectations on the project. In case a project manager does run into such situations, then my recommendation would be to temporarily put a hold on the project until the scope issue has been addressed and fixed, after which the project can restart from where it left off.

Do project managers write project proposals?

Companies usually hire project managers to execute projects once the budget and the project charter has been reviewed and approved by the project management office also known as the PMO. The PMO also employs a group of project managers whose primary function is to work on proposals, processes and performance metrics. They also keep a tab on active projects to make sure they are on track with respect to scope, cost, performance, and quality.

In some cases, project managers are

assigned to preparing project proposals and to also work with management on budget and project justification, which is usually part of another group called the project pipeline management. The project is then assigned to an execution project manager after the budget and scope of work is approved by the business.

It is important to highlight that project contract and procurement management are part of the project management function and the guidelines are well documented in the PMBOK, published by the PMI (Project Management Institute).

When it comes to vendor contracts, it is usually managed by the vendor management department. They usually coordinate with the technical and/or business team that is requiring vendor support. The vendor management team within the organization houses experts that can negotiate contracts from a scope, pricing and delivery perspective. Once the contract is established, the project manager and the team involved work directly with the vendor contact in terms of tasks and delivery responsibilities.

Scope change leading to budget impacts

I can say with certainty that scope change is inevitable in any project environment. In order to deal with competition, companies have to make rapid business changes and this is going to affect all or some of the triple constraints (Scope, Schedule, Cost) on one or more projects. What we are going to address here is the cost impact of a potential scope change.

In most cases, a budget is assigned to a program and a portion of that budget is allocated to the project. This usually happens prior to project kickoff and I would call that the high-level cost estimate for high-level scope of work. The high-level cost estimate is usually considered a ballpark only because the details of the scope has not been drawn up as yet and what I mean by that is the completion of requirements and design phase. Remember that when we talk about cost estimate, it is cumulative of both internal and external costs (e.g., vendor).

The project manager usually goes back to the internal and external teams after the requirements and design phase; handing over a copy of the approved requirements so that the teams can true-up the final costs. The cumulative total of the cost estimates now becomes the total cost of the project against which progress will be measured at execution. Any potential scope change at this point or later will result in a change request that can affect both the scope and budget.

In some organizations, task estimate is calculated based on hourly rate and how long the resource is expected to be work on a project. Of course, vendor work can be either calculated as a rate per hour of work or they may have agreed to a fixed price contract. Either way when the scope changes, the budget is impacted and therefore a change request approval process is a must to record and document such changes to the project for a future audit and performance review on a completed project.

PMP versus Agile Certification

PMP certification from PMI is still popular and sought after in many organizations. Remember that project management theory and PMBOK still provide the fundamental foundation for successful project management. As a far as I can tell, there are still a number of companies small, medium and large that are using the traditional waterfall model or a combination of traditional and agile. Further, PMP certification also provides a good foundation for moving to agile and acquiring the agile project certification.

Nature and complexity of the industry can also be a reason for an organization to stay with the traditional approach. For example, in the telecommunication space, there are massive projects that does not lend itself well to an agile development methodology. In some cases, the individual teams are big, along with vendors supporting and implementing work worth millions of dollars that also includes massive infrastructure deployments.

In my view, at some point in the future, it is very much possible that agile will take over all of development. We are seeing other variations of agile being introduced in the market combined with a host of new certifications. Some of the new technologies may completely go agile to take advantage of the speed and efficiency it brings to development and implementation.

Task estimation on projects - challenges

In my opinion, estimation is more an art than a science. There is no right or wrong approach to estimation. If a team member is able to accurately describe and break down his/her scope of work, then the estimate is likely to be close to the actual work hours when the task is completed. When receiving estimates, the project manager always has to assume some variation say 10 to 15% in order to account for unanticipated or unplanned work.

Based on places that I have worked, I can tell for sure that architects, analysts, and developers have not been trained enough on how to estimate work. Each team has a different approach to estimation, which means there is a lack of standard when approaching the estimation process. In my view, it should be the responsibility of the project management office (PMO) to establish the necessary tools and processes to enforce a consistent approach to estimation so that it is an orange-to-orange comparison between teams and across projects. Historical data from past projects can also be used as a guidepost for estimation of project tasks.

As a project manager, one will also notice that there is little consistency in the way the tasks and estimates are provided the project teams. Some teams provided high-level tasks and some others provide detailed tasks and subtasks. Other teams may provide task dependencies and/or resource names, hours etc. My point here is that the PMO or the responsible project manager should be able to guide the team members with the support of the department heads. There is often a push back on the framework and the approach because it is more work for those teams in additional to doing the assigned work. It is also important for the teams to realize that the success of the overall project is dependent on managing and controlling every aspect of the project based on some fundamental project management principles.

The politics of managing projects

Politics is an integral part of any institution organized around people. It takes an even important place when there is contention for resources and that means the most powerful and influential person wins. Similarly, in a projectized organization project managers and departments are fighting for resources that are limited. It naturally forces the project manager to schedule work around those constraints as well as build relationships to have better influence over such demands.

While most of us may think that diplomacy is the answer, it is important for a project manager to escalate and get support from the reporting manager and the PMO to find solutions to project problems. They will help to find the balance by talking to the necessary department heads, to size up the work based on some form of prioritization so that those resources are available for all critical projects. One other venue for escalation is the weekly risk meeting and can be a great forum to help mitigate such related issues. The risk meeting brings together project managers, PMO, department heads and sometimes senior management and can be treated as a one stop-shop to resolve such issues.

This is a skill that one cannot be taught. It is something that comes from experience, but that is not guaranteed. A project manager may falter in the process because it is difficult sometimes due to the toxic nature of the environment. A project manager has better odds of success in an organization that is focused on support and collaboration. In some cases, it can also be a natural skill that comes from life experiences and family upbringing.

To conclude, I can tell with confidence that political maneuverability can be a great asset to a project manager in terms of driving successful project outcomes in the face of many unforeseen environmental challenges.

Theory versus practical project mgmt. - gaps

As a reminder, this question is all about that perceived gap. When a project manager walks into a job interview, he/she has to expect that most of the questions are going to be around specific project situations. However, successfully responding to those questions may not mean anything to you until you start working in that environment. To clarify, it is the difference between what you know and expect versus what you are going to experience in the new job environment.

In my view, if you have read the PMBOK and have a commonsensical understanding of project management principles, it is easy to get through the interview process so long as you can articulate and communicate the stated question. Assuming you get selected, it still does not guarantee with what you would have expected on the job. That could mean new processes, new systems, new people, methodology, communication protocol etc. Culture plays a big factor if not the most important challenge that will require understanding and personal adjustment.

Many in the managerial space fail to realize that it takes at a minimum 3-6 months before a project manager gets adjusted to the environment. In some cases, it is unfortunate that the contract comes to close either because of the budget or the project manager has not met performance objectives as defined by the PMO or the management. Now the project manager has to start from ground up and this is a vicious circle for any project manager or consultant and something he/she should be ready to face.

I strongly believe that success is a two-way street. The organization has a responsibility to also ensure that the project manager will be successful in the new environment. In the same token, I want commend organizations that have done a great job of making a home for the new project manager, and those are places where the project manager has stayed longer with the organization leading to excellent job performance and satisfaction.

PMBOK adoption and practical project management

During the initial years as a project manager, after acquiring PMP certification, I was under the assumption that I would see and experience many of the guidelines and best practices that is presented in the PMBOK document. To my surprise, the reality on the ground was completely different. There is a notion in the project management universe that PMBOK is only a guideline document for implementing project management. An organization can design, develop and implement their own methodology using the PMBOK as a guideline. However, based on my experience only 20-25% of the PMBOK methodology is actually implemented resulting in frequent project failures and other related inefficiencies.

I also want to clear the myth that implementing the PMBOK does not guarantee success, but the odds of success are likely to increase by adopting more of the PMBOK guidelines. With little or no application of PMBOK, problems and issues on projects can increase and significantly alter the outcome leading to increased costs on the project.

To conclude, I am not sure about the application of agile project management, but maybe there is better adoption in this case. What I said about PMBOK equally applies to the agile space as well. The PMBOK can provide a great foundation for agile implementation in organizations.

Future of project management

In my view, the future of project management is bright. As I had mentioned in one of my previous responses, traditional project management is here to stay for a while because it provides a foundation for effective project management. There are still companies using the traditional project management approach to support large and complex projects. Organizational culture is also affecting the migration to an agile environment.

Most companies today have adopted management by projects and that is a testament to the success of the project management. Project management is gaining traction in the agile world and therefore it is here to stay. It is imperative that project managers acquire necessary certification and experience in agile methodology to stay relevant.

In addition to staying relevant in project management, it is also critical to gain experience in the technical space. Gaining experience and exposure to areas such as cloud computing, data science, machine learning, and predictive analytics can provide a head start when companies are looking for technical project managers. Platform-specific experience such as SAP,

SaaS, and SalesForce can also give a project manager market advantage over a generalist or functional project manager.

A project manager may be at risk of employment if he/she is a generalist or a functional project manager. Having functional experience (Insurance, Finance) can be an added benefit so long as he/she has technical credentials.

Project manager - skills & attributes

I would put this differently. What skills, traits, and attributes would help someone like the roles and responsibilities of a project manager? Here is a list and there could be more:

- Likes to manage people
- Enjoys leadership and wants to lead teams
- Is passionate and enthusiastic about the function and principles of project management

- Likes to motivate teams and individual members
- Enjoys and challenges himself/herself on the politics of project management.
- Is passionate about the organization and its structure.
- Looking for visibility and related growth.
- Strongly believes that project management can greatly help an organization deliver products and services.
- Willing to take on the challenges associated with project management.
- Is willing to work on delivery projects on schedule and on budget.

- Willing to communicate and deal with risks and issues on a timely basis.

Organizations may add other job requirements, but what I listed above is only a starting point for identifying good project managers. Most of the attributes can be learned only by experience, but chances of failure is equally high if a project manager oversteps the boundaries that are defined by his/her place of work or the job.

Organizational culture - impact on project manager

If a project manager is employed in a startup or a small scale company, he/she will notice that the project management framework is not as robust or mature as one would have hoped. There could be a couple of reasons that are as follows:

- The company is fairly new and is scaling up on the technology front with limited or no budget for project management.

- Project management work is always considered an overhead or the cost of doing business and therefore the organization does not see the value behind it.
- The company wants to a take a quick and easy route to implementing products/services with minimal oversight and management .

In these conditions, a project manager has the opportunity to grow the project management practice by convincing the senior management about its inherent benefits. The other option will be to develop a project methodology framework with what is available and grow that practice as soon as the company has grown to a certain level or has acquired a set number of clients that will demand a more effective execution and delivery approach.

References

- PMI is a registered trademark of Project Management Institute. www.pmi.org
- CAPM (Certified Associate in Project Management) is a professional certification offered by the Project Management Institute.
- PMP (Project Management Professional) is a professional certification offered by the Project Management Institute.
- PMBOK (a.k.a Project Management Book of Knowledge) is solely owned by the Project Management Institute.
- PMI-ACP (Agile Certified Practitioner) is a professional certification offered by the Project Management Institute.
- Microsoft Project is a registered property of Microsoft.

- Microsoft Office is a registered property of Microsoft.
- Lotus Notes is a registered property of IBM / Lenovo.
- ITIL is a registered property of AXELOS
- Clarity is a registered property of CA Technologies.

www.ingramcontent.com/pod-product-compliance
Lightning Source LLC
Chambersburg PA
CBHW052257220526
45471CB00001B/372